# Big Book of Things to Make and Do

## Anna Milbourne and Rebecca Gilpin

Edited by Sarah Khan

Designed by Helen Edmonds, Non Figg and Amanda Gulliver

Illustrated by Stephen Cartwright and Molly Sage

Photographs by Howard Allman

Additional material by Catherine Atkinson, Ruth Brocklehurst,
Kate Knighton, Minna Lacey, Leonie Pratt and Fiona Watt

Additional designs by Katrina Fearn, Erica Harrison,
Michelle Lawrence, Jan McCafferty and Josephine Thompson

Image credit: p.29 © Juniors Bildarchiv/Alamy
Digital manipulation by Nick Wakeford and Will Dawes

First published in 2008 by Usborne Publishing Ltd, Usborne House, 83-85 Saffron Hill, London ECIN 8RT, England.
www.usborne.com  Copyright © 2008 Usborne Publishing Ltd. The name Usborne and the devices ♛ ⊕ are Trade Marks of Usborne
First published in America 2008. U.E. Printed in China.

# Contents

There are little yellow ducks hidden throughout the book.
When you have found a duck, you can put
a 🦆 sticker on the page.

This is Apple Tree Farm.

Mr. and Mrs. Boot live here with
their two children, Poppy and Sam.
They have a dog called Rusty and a cat
called Whiskers. Ted drives the tractor
and helps out on the farm.

# Poppy's paper daisy chains

Make all the stems go off the sides of the paper.

1. Fold a rectangle of white paper in half so that the two shorter edges meet. Then, fold it in half again.

2. Draw a daisy near the top of the folded paper. Add a thick stem on each side. Draw two more daisies underneath.

3. Using a pair of scissors, cut around the daisies, but don't cut along the folds at the ends of the stems.

4. Open out your daisy chains. Using a yellow felt-tip pen, draw on spots for the middles of the daisies.

Add the edges of the petals before you fill in the stems.

5. Fill in the stems using a green felt-tip pen. Then, tape your daisy chains together to make one long chain.

# Cut-out farm animals

1. Fold a rectangle of thick white paper about the size of this page in half so that the two shorter edges meet. Press along the fold.

2. Draw a straight line about a finger's width from the bottom. Fold the paper inward along the line. Do the same on the other side.

3. Draw a cow on the folded paper, like this. Make its back go along the top fold and its feet go all the way to the bottom.

Don't cut along this side.

Don't cut here.

4. Cut out the cow shape, cutting through both sides of the folded paper. Don't cut along its back or the bottom of its feet.

5. Turn the folded paper over and draw the cow on the blank side too. Fill it in on both sides of the paper using felt-tip pens.

6. Cut out a small rectangle of thick green paper. Spread glue onto the folds under the cow's feet and press them onto the green paper.

You can make more animals in the same way, to create your own farmyard.

# Growing shoots

If you don't have any beans, you can use dried chickpeas instead.

1. Put four dried beans into a small bowl. Pour water on top to cover them. Leave them for about half an hour.

2. Soak a jar in warm soapy water. Peel off the label. Rinse the jar with cold water. Leave it wet on the inside.

3. Scrunch up a paper towel. Wrap a bright paper napkin around the scrunched-up towel to make a bundle.

4. Push the bundle into the jar. Hold the napkin away from the side, then push a bean down between the jar and the napkin.

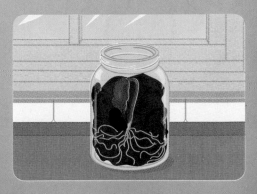

A sunny windowsill is a good place to grow your beans.

5. Place the other three beans around the side of the jar in the same way. Press the napkin back against the jar.

6. Spoon some water into the jar, until the napkin is fairly wet. Then, put the jar in a warm, bright place.

7. Spoon more water into the jar each day, to keep the napkin wet. After a few days, shoots will begin to grow.

# Planting your shoot

Make the hole big enough to hold your shoot's roots.

Water the shoot every few days.

1. Put small stones in a plant pot with a hole in it. Fill the pot almost to the top with compost. Make a hole in the compost.

2. Lift a shoot out of the jar. Hold it upright in the pot and add compost around it. Press the compost down.

It takes about two weeks for beans and chickpeas to grow into shoots like these.

You could decorate your jar using a strip of green paper and stickers from the sticker pages.

When your shoot starts to grow over the top of the jar, it's big enough to plant in soil.

# Egg toppers

These crowns were cut from shiny paper and decorated with sequins and glitter glue.

## Pointed hat

You only need one half for the hat.

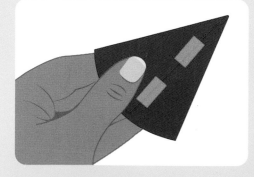

1. Lay a small plate on a piece of paper and draw around it. Cut out the circle and fold it in half. Then, cut along the fold.

2. Bend the paper around so that the corners overlap and make a cone. Then, secure the edges with small pieces of sticky tape.

## Crown

Make all the triangles the same size.

Cut a paper strip that will fit around an egg. Draw triangles along the top, then cut them out. Bend the paper around and tape the ends.

# Pirate hat

1. Cut a piece of paper about 12x15cm (5x6in). Fold it in half so that the short ends are together and the fold is at the top.

The mark shows where the middle is.

2. Bend the paper in half and pinch the corner to make a mark. Unfold the paper and fold the corners into the middle, like this.

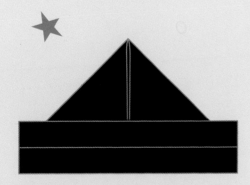

3. Fold up the top layer of paper at the bottom of the hat. Then, turn the hat over and fold the paper on that side up in the same way.

The skull and crossbones on this pirate hat were cut from paper and glued on.

# Hanging butterflies

## Salt speckled butterflies

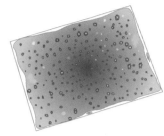

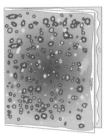

1. Paint all over a sheet of thick white paper with watery paint. Then, sprinkle grains of salt onto the paint and let it dry.

2. When the paint is dry, brush off the salt. Fold the paper in half and glue it together with the paint on the outside.

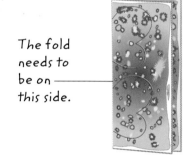

The fold needs to be on this side.

3. Fold the paper in half again. Draw two butterfly wings on it, then cut around the wings, through all the layers of paper.

4. For each butterfly, cut the end off a drinking straw, just above the bumpy part. To make feelers, cut down into the bumpy part.

Snip here.

Make sure the bead is wider than the straw.

5. Bend the feelers outward, then open the wings. Lay the straw in the fold, then snip off the bottom end of the straw.

6. Push a piece of ribbon through a bead. Tie a knot in the ribbon and push it through the straw. Glue the straw onto the wings.

Make lots of butterflies, then hang them up.

# Splattered butterflies

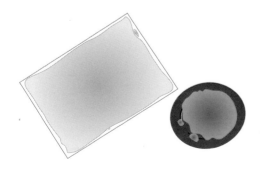

1. Paint all over a sheet of thick white paper with watery paint and let it dry. Then, put some bright paint onto an old plate.

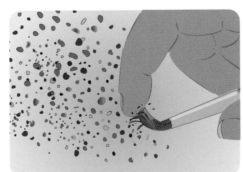

2. Dip a dry paintbrush into the paint, then hold it over the paper. Pull a finger over the bristles, to splatter the paint.

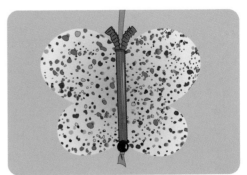

3. Splatter the paint all over the paper and let it dry. Then, make two butterflies, following the steps on the opposite page.

# Mrs. Boot's decorated pots

## Spotted pot

1. Wash a terracotta flower pot thoroughly with water, to remove any soil. Then, leave the pot overnight to dry out completely.

*Paint inside the top, too.*

2. Paint the outside of the pot with white acrylic paint. Leave the paint to dry, then paint some light purple circles on the pot.

*Make the circles different sizes.*

3. Paint darker purple and yellow circles in the spaces. Then, paint more circles on top and leave the paint to dry.

*You could decorate a base, too.*

Put a pretty plant in the pot.

# Flowery pot

1. Wash a flower pot, let it dry, then paint it pale pink. Cut some circles and petal shapes from different shades of thin paper.

Use a glue stick.

2. Glue some of the petals onto the pot to make a flower. Then, glue a circle in the middle of the flower and add another flower.

The glue is clear when it dries.

3. Paint a thick layer of white glue all over the outside of the pot, including the paper flowers. Leave the glue to dry.

# Mrs. Boot's birthday card

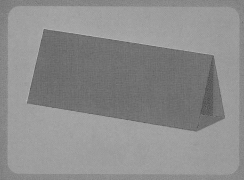

*Make the stalks all different heights.*

1. To make a long thin card, fold a rectangular piece of thick yellow paper in half so that the two longer edges meet. Press along the fold.

2. Draw seven tulip shapes on bright paper. Carefully cut them out. Then, draw seven long stalks on a piece of green paper and cut them out, too.

3. Glue the stalks onto the card, letting them overlap the bottom edge. Use a pair of scissors to trim the ends off. Glue the tulips onto the stalks.

# Whiskers bookmark

1. On a piece of white paper, draw a cat's head and two paws, like this. Fill them in with felt-tip pens.

2. Cut around the shape. Put it on top of another piece of thick paper and draw around it using a pencil.

You don't need to fill in this part.

3. Add a cat's body under the pencil outline and fill it in with felt-tip pens. Cut around the whole cat shape.

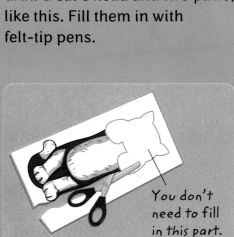

4. Spread glue on the top part of the head. Then, press the filled-in head shape on top, lining up the ears.

Leave your bookmark to dry before you use it.

Hook the cat's paws over a page to mark your place in a book.

# Caterpillar and flowers

## Caterpillar

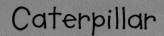

You don't need the lid.

1. Carefully cut the lid off a cardboard egg carton. Then, cut the bottom part of the carton into two pieces, along its length.

2. To make the caterpillar, paint one piece green, and leave it to dry. Put the other piece to one side, for the flowers.

3. Carefully push the point of a ballpoint pen into the front of the caterpillar to make two holes for its feelers.

You could paint spots instead of using stickers.

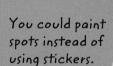

4. Push two short pieces of drinking straw through the holes. Then, draw a face. Press stickers all over the caterpillar's body.

# Flowers

1. For the middles of the flowers, cut the other piece of egg carton into three pieces. Paint them orange and let them dry.

2. Draw a petal on thin cardboard and cut it out. Then, draw around it lots of times on bright paper and cut out the shapes.

*Make the flowers with different petal shapes.*

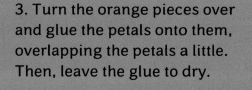

3. Turn the orange pieces over and glue the petals onto them, overlapping the petals a little. Then, leave the glue to dry.

4. Tear a piece of yellow tissue paper into three pieces. Scrunch them up, then glue them into the middles of the orange sections.

5. For the stalks, press a piece of poster tack onto the back of each flower. Then, press a straw firmly into the poster tack.

# Dangly scarecrow

Keep the other semicircle to use later.

1. Put a plate onto a piece of thick blue paper. Draw around it using a pencil. Then, carefully cut out the circle.

2. Fold the circle in half and then open it out again. Carefully cut along the fold to make two semicircles.

3. Spread some glue about halfway along the flat edge of one of the semicircles, like this.

Hold the edges in place until they stick.

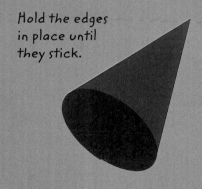

Make the string about five times the length of the cone.

This loop is for hanging your scarecrow up.

You may need to snip the tip off the cone with a pair of scissors.

4. Holding the straight edge, bend the semicircle around to make a cone. Then, press the edges together.

5. Cut a long piece of string. Fold it in half. Then, tie a knot near the folded end to make a loop.

6. Push the string up through the cone, so that the loop pokes out of the top and the knot is inside.

Draw little lines around his nose so that it looks stitched on.

7. Draw a scarecrow's face on a piece of thick white paper. Add a hat and hair. Fill them in. Then, cut it out.

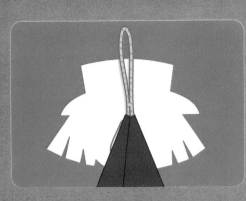

8. Put a blob of glue on the back of the scarecrow's head. Press the head onto the cone body.

This will make two shoes.

9. Fold the leftover blue semicircle in half. Draw a shoe shape. Then cut it out through both layers of paper.

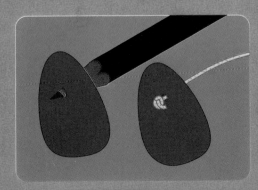

10. Using a pencil, poke a hole in each shoe. Push the string through the shoe and tie a knot in the bottom.

You could make a crow, too. To make a smaller cone, use a cup instead of a plate to draw the circle.

You could draw pockets and buttons on the scarecrow's coat.

21

# Hand-print crow

1. Pour some black paint onto the front sheet of an old newspaper. Then, spread the paint out with a paintbrush.

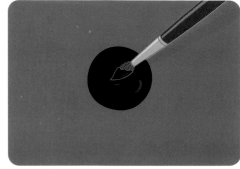

2. Paint a crow's round head near the top of a big piece of paper. Make it almost as wide as your hand.

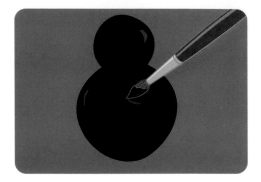

3. Dip your brush into the black paint again and paint a big, fat body underneath the crow's head.

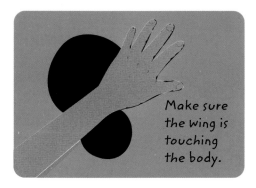

Make sure the wing is touching the body.

4. Turn your picture upside down. Dip your hand into the paint and press it onto the paper to print a wing.

5. Dip your other hand into the paint. Press it down on the other side of the body to print another wing.

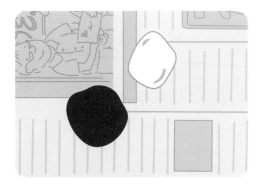

6. Wash your hands. Then, pour a little orange paint and a little white paint onto some more old newspaper.

Turn your crow back the right way around.

7. Dip a clean brush into the orange paint and paint a beak on your crow. Add his legs and feet too.

8. Dip the tip of your finger into the white paint. Press it onto the crow's head to make an eye. Let it dry.

9. Dip the tip of your little finger into the black paint. Press it into the middle of the white circle.

# Fingerprint sheep card

Rinse the spoon so you don't mix the paints.

1. To make a card, fold a piece of thick yellow paper in half so that the two shorter edges meet. Press along the fold.

2. Cut a rectangle of green paper, a little smaller than your card. Spread glue on the back and then press it onto the front of your card.

3. Put two paper towels on top of an old newspaper. Pour a little white and yellow paint on top. Spread the paint out with a spoon.

4. Dip the tip of your finger into the white paint. Press it onto the card to make a fingerprint. Add lots more to make a sheep's body.

5. Dip your thumb into the paint. Make a thumbprint for the sheep's face. Add some more fingerprints on top of the sheep's head.

6. Once the paint is dry, use a black felt-tip pen to draw two dots for the sheep's eyes. Then, add its nose, ears and legs.

7. Dip your finger into the yellow paint to make little fingerprinted flowers on the grass. Add white fingerprints for their middles.

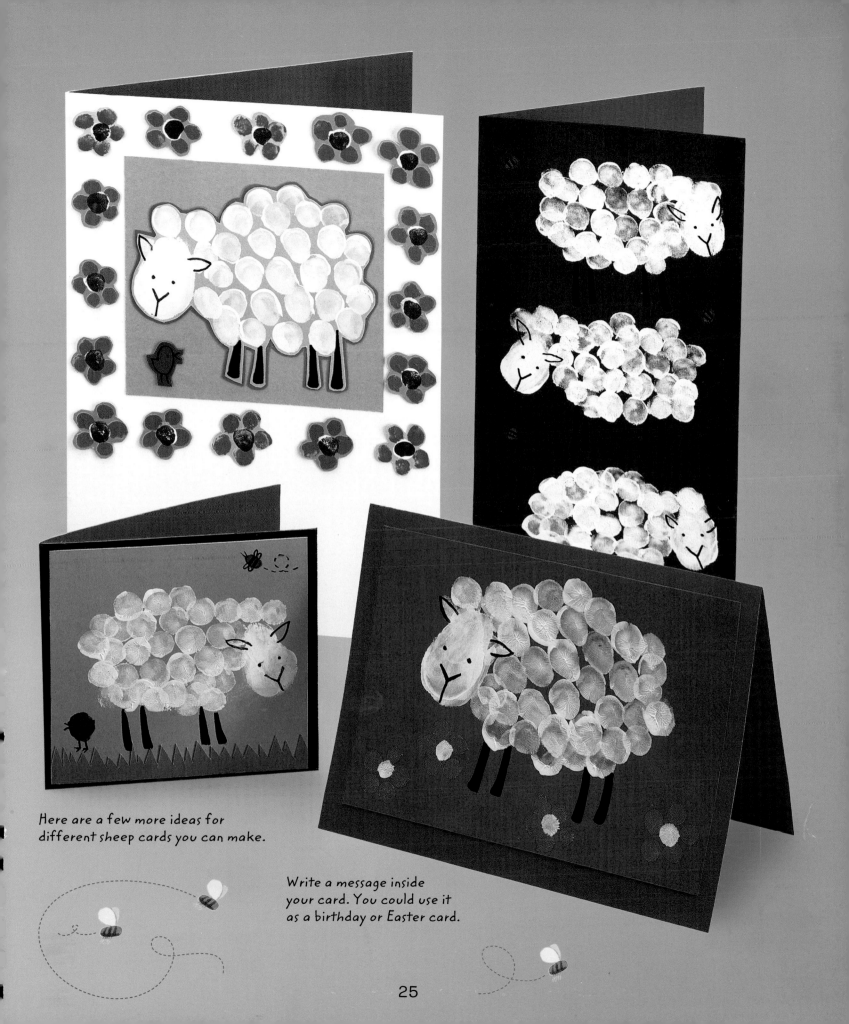

Here are a few more ideas for different sheep cards you can make.

Write a message inside your card. You could use it as a birthday or Easter card.

# Poppy and Sam's decorated eggs

To make six decorated eggs, you'll need:

6 eggs at room temperature
food dye
wax crayons
tiny star-shaped stickers
rubber bands

The eggs need to be stored in a refrigerator and eaten within three days.

## Cooking the eggs

Use a slotted spoon.

1. Put the eggs into a pan of cold water. Heat the pan. When the water is gently boiling, reduce the heat.

2. Cook the eggs for eight to nine minutes. Then, lift them out and put them in a bowl of cold water to cool.

## Wax patterns

The wax resists the food dye.

Leave the egg for about 10 minutes.

1. Use a wax crayon to draw patterns on a dry egg. Put 3-4 teaspoons of bright food dye into a glass.

2. Half fill the glass with water. Put the egg into the glass. Using a spoon, turn the egg to dye it all over.

3. When the egg is brightly dyed, lift it out of the glass with a spoon. Put the egg on a paper towel to dry.

## Stripes

1. Stretch a thick rubber band around a dry egg. Stretch one around the egg from the top to the bottom.

2. Add more rubber bands. Dye the egg as before and let it dry. Remove the bands to see the stripes of eggshell.

The rabbits and chicks were painted straight onto the eggs with food dye.

# Stickers

Make sure the egg is dry.

1. Press tiny stickers onto an egg. Use shiny ones if you can, as they don't soak up so much food dye.

2. Dye the egg in a glass, as before. Then, lift the egg out with a spoon and put it on a paper towel to dry.

3. When the egg is dry, peel off the stickers. You'll see the shade of the eggshell where the stickers were.

# Garden things
## Poppy's bug viewer

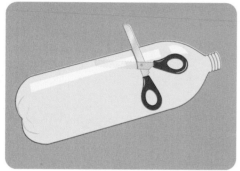

1. Carefully cut the top third off a plastic bottle. Then, place it upside down in the bottom part of the bottle.

2. Use a small spade or shovel to scoop garden soil, dead plants and leaves into the top part of the bottle.

3. Leave the bug viewer under a bright lamp for an hour. Any bugs in the soil will drop into the lower part.

4. Look at the bugs through a magnifying glass. Then, gently pour the bugs out onto the ground where you found them.

*Another good way to collect bugs is to leave half an orange upside down on the soil overnight. The next day, you might find bugs inside it.*

# Hanging bird feeder

1. Pour unsalted peanuts into a plastic net, almost to the top. Then, tie a knot at the top.

2. Thread some string through the top of the net, like this. Then, hang it up.

# Peanut string

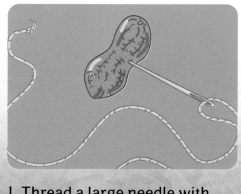

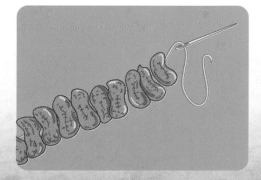

1. Thread a large needle with string and tie a knot in the end. Push the needle through a peanut shell.

2. Push the needle through several more peanut shells. Leave enough string at the end to hang them up.

# Fish picture

Make each strip as fat as three fingers.

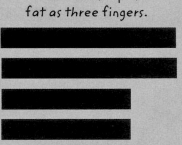

1. Cut two strips of thick blue paper about the length of this page. Then cut two more strips about the width of this page.

2. Spread glue on both ends of one of the short strips. Press the long strips onto it. Glue on the other short strip to make a frame.

3. Put your frame on top of a piece of blue tissue paper and draw around it to make a rectangle. Cut around the rectangle carefully.

Use an old paintbrush to spread the glue.

Don't make any of the strips longer than your frame.

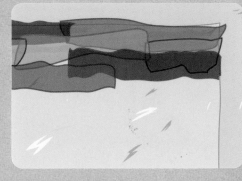

4. Rip some different shades of blue tissue paper into strips. Lay them on top of a piece of food wrap and spread glue onto them.

5. Lay the tissue paper rectangle on top of another piece of food wrap. Press the strips onto it, going across the paper, like this.

6. Spread glue onto your frame. Then press it on top of the tissue paper rectangle, taking care to line up the edges.

These fish have tails and fins made out of different shades of tissue paper.

You can fill your picture with as many fish as you like. This one has lots of little fish.

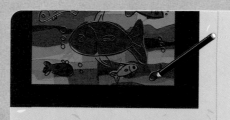

Your outlines don't have to follow the edges of the tissue shapes.

7. Rip some little oval shapes out of bright tissue paper. Spread glue onto them. Press them onto the tissue paper in the frame.

8. Leave the picture to dry. Use a black felt-tip pen to draw fish on top of the tissue shapes. Add air bubbles from their mouths.

9. Carefully peel your tissue fish picture off the food wrap. Hang it up in a window, so that the light shines through it.

# Farmyard cookies

To make about 18 cookies, you'll need:

350g (12oz, 2 cups) plain or all-purpose flour
2 teaspoons of ground ginger
1 teaspoon of bicarbonate of soda or 2 teaspoons
  of baking soda
100g (4oz, ½ cup, 1 stick) butter
175g (6oz, 1 cup) soft light brown sugar
1 egg
4 tablespoons of golden or corn syrup
large farm animal cookie cutters

Preheat your oven to 180°C, 350°F,
Gas Mark 4

Keep in an airtight container and eat within five days.

1. Dip a paper towel in some margarine and rub it over two baking trays to grease them. Then, turn on your oven.

2. Sift the flour, ginger and soda into a large mixing bowl. Cut the butter into chunks and add it to the bowl.

3. Rub the butter into the flour with your fingertips, until the mixture looks like fine breadcrumbs. Then, stir in the sugar.

4. Break the egg into a small bowl. Add the syrup to the egg. Using a fork, beat the syrup and egg together well.

5. Stir the eggy mixture into the flour. Mix everything together with a metal spoon until it makes a soft dough.

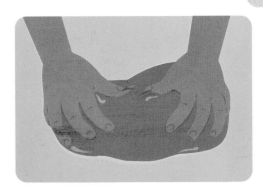

6. Sprinkle a clean work surface with flour and put the dough onto it. Stretch the dough by pushing it away from you.

7. Fold the dough in half. Turn it and push it away from you again. Continue to push, turn and fold until the dough is smooth.

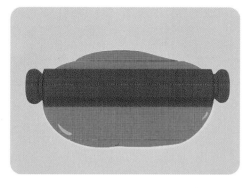

8. Cut the dough in half. Sprinkle a little more flour onto your work surface. Roll out the dough until it is about 5mm (¼in) thick.

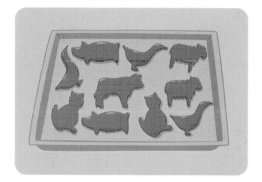

9. Use cookie cutters to cut out lots of shapes from the dough. Then, lift the shapes onto the baking trays with a spatula.

10. Roll out the other half of dough and cut shapes from it. Squeeze the scraps to make a ball. Roll it out and cut more shapes.

Spread the shapes out on the baking trays.

11. Put the baking trays into your oven and bake them for 12-15 minutes until they have turned golden brown.

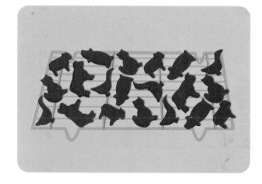

12. Leave the cookies on the sheets for about five minutes. Then, lift them onto a wire rack. Leave them to cool.

# Piggy picture frame

*Make each strip as fat as three of your fingers.*

1. Cut two strips of thick yellow paper a little longer than this page and two more strips about the width of this page.

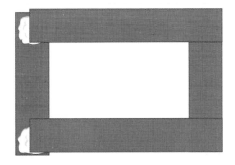

2. Spread glue on both ends of one of the short strips. Press the long strips onto it. Glue on the other short strip to make a frame.

You can tape a picture to the back of the frame.

*If you don't have pink paint, mix some white and red paint together.*

3. Pour a little pink paint onto a plate. Dip your finger into the paint. Press it onto the frame to print a pig's body. Print lots more.

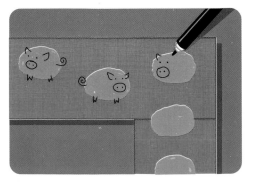

4. Let the paint dry. Then use a black felt-tip pen to draw the pigs' eyes, ears and snouts. Add their legs and give them each a curly tail.

# Marzipan rabbits

To make 6 rabbits, you'll need:

a 100g (4oz) block of marzipan*

red food dye

a toothpick

The rabbits need to be stored in an airtight container and eaten within three weeks.

* Marzipan contains ground nuts, so don't give these to anyone who is allergic to nuts.

1. Mix one drop of red food dye into the marzipan with your fingers until it has turned pink.

2. Cut the marzipan in half. With one half, make six balls for the bodies. Cut the other piece in half

3. From one half of the marzipan, roll six small balls. These will be the rabbits' heads.

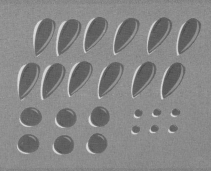

4. From the other half of the marzipan, make twelve ears, six tails and six noses.

*If the ears won't stick, dip the ends in water.*

5. Fold the ears. Press the ears, heads, noses and tails onto the bodies. Press eyes with a toothpick.

*Press a rabbit's head on the front of its body, to make it look as if it is lying down.*

# Sam's froggy door sign

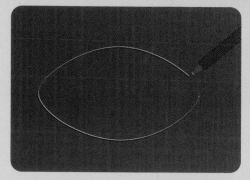

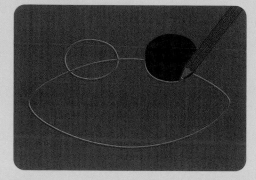

Use the side without pencil marks as the front of the frog's head.

1. Draw a big leaf shape for the frog's head on a piece of green paper. Make the leaf shape about as wide as this page.

2. Draw around a small jar lid to make two big eye shapes on top of his head. Then, carefully cut around your frog's head.

3. Cut a big round shape for the body. It doesn't have to be perfectly round. Make it a little narrower than the head.

The short strips are the frog's arms.

The long strips are the frog's legs.

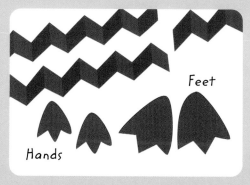

Feet

Hands

This is the back of the frog.

4. Cut three strips of paper, each about 30cm (12in) long. Fold one strip in half. Cut along the fold to make two shorter strips.

5. Fold each strip lots of times to make zigzags. Draw two hands and two feet on a piece of green paper and cut them out.

6. Tape the head onto the body. Then, tape the arms and legs onto the body. Tape the hands and feet onto the arms and legs.

These will be the frog's eyes.

7. Put a small jar lid on a piece of white paper. Draw around it to make two circles. Fill in their middles with a felt-tip pen. Cut them out.

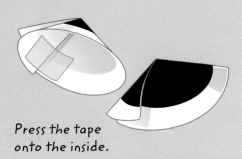

*Press the tape onto the inside.*

8. Snip into the middle of each circle. Pull the cut edges in so they overlap, making a shallow cone, and tape them in place.

*Press the tape on, then let the eye fold down.*

9. Cut another piece of tape. Press one end inside a cone eye, and the other end onto the frog's head. Tape the other eye on like this, too.

10. Using a black felt-tip pen, draw nostrils and a big smile on your frog. Write your name on its tummy and hang it on your bedroom door.

Sam's room

*If you want your frog to have a pale tummy like this one, glue it on before you tape on the frog's head.*

# Poppy's glittery crown

1. Cut a long rectangle of thin cardboard that fits around your head, with a little overlap. Then, draw a line across the middle of it.

Make the crosses taller than the points. Leave a plain part at each end.

2. Draw points and crosses along the line, like this. Cut out the crown shape, then paint it gold or silver on both sides.

Slit

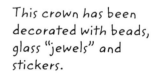

3. When the paint is dry, cut a slit going down, a little way from one end. Then, make another slit going up, near the other end.

4. Bring the ends of the crown together. Slot them in place, with the ends inside, like this. Then, secure the ends with tape.

5. Cut eight little hearts from red paper and glue them to the crown. For a fur trim, glue cotton balls along the bottom.

This crown has been decorated with beads, glass "jewels" and stickers.

You can make differently shaped crowns, like this, too.

This part is messy, so work on old newspapers.

6. For jewels, roll eight pieces of foil into little balls. Cover the balls with white glue and roll them in glitter.

You will need to crumple the paper a little as you tape it.

7. Leave the jewels until they are completely dry. Then, glue them at equal spaces on the fur around the bottom of the crown.

8. Place a large plate on a piece of red crêpe paper or tissue paper and draw around it. Then, cut out the circle.

9. Push the middle of the circle through the crown from the bottom. Tape the edge of the circle inside the crown, like this.

# Leaf-print butterflies

Use the back of the spoon.

1. Put a piece of sponge cloth on top of an old newspaper. Pour a little paint on top. Spread it out with an old spoon.

Leaves with veins that stick out make good prints.

2. Press a leaf onto the sponge cloth, with the veins facing down. Then, press it onto a piece of paper and peel it off to make a print.

3. Make three more leaf prints on the same piece of paper. Leave them to dry. Then, carefully cut around them.

Make the body the same length as your leaf.

This will be the back of your butterfly.

4. Cut a long shape for the butterfly's body from bright paper. Put a blob of glue on the front of a leaf print and press it onto the body.

5. Glue the other three leaf shapes onto the body, like this, so they look like butterfly wings. Leave the glue to dry.

These butterflies have been decorated with sequins.

You can use stickers from the sticker pages to decorate your butterflies.

These are the feelers.

6. Cut two thin strips of paper as long as your finger. Roll up the ends to make them curl. Tape them onto the back of the head.

7. Turn your butterfly over. Use a felt-tip pen to draw its mouth and eyes. Then, decorate its wings with glitter glue or shiny stickers.

# Toadstool picture

Use the back of an old spoon.

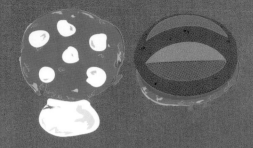

1. Lay some paper towels on some newspaper. Spread red or pink paint on the paper towels with a spoon.

2. Cut a potato in half. Cut away the two sides, like this, to make a handle. Press the potato into the paint.

3. Press the potato on a piece of paper. Fingerpaint white dots onto the print. Using a brush, paint a white stalk.

# Daisies and dandelions

1. Cut two small pieces of thick cardboard. To print daisies, dip the edge of one piece in white paint and press it on the paper.

2. Print lots more lines and cross them over each other, to make petals. Then, paint a yellow dot in the middle of each daisy.

3. Dip the long edge of the other piece of cardboard in yellow paint and print dandelions. Then, paint stalks and leaves.

# Dragonflies

1. To paint a body, dip a fingertip into some paint and drag your finger quickly across the paper. Then, fingerpaint a head.

2. Clean your finger, then dip it in some white paint and drag it to make four wings. Then, add eyes with a felt-tip pen.

*Print some toadstools first, then add flowers in the spaces.*

# Poppy and Sam's paper kite

*Make sure the fold is on the left, like this.*

*You could fold the paper over a ruler, to help you get it straight.*

1. Fold a rectangular piece of fairly thin paper in half so that the two shorter sides meet. Press along the fold.

2. Make a pencil mark two fingers' width from the top left corner. Make another the same distance from the bottom right corner.

3. Using a ruler, draw a pencil line joining up the two marks. Then fold the paper along the line, like this. Press it flat.

4. Turn the folded paper over. Then, fold the top piece back so that it matches the other side. Press along the fold, then open it out again.

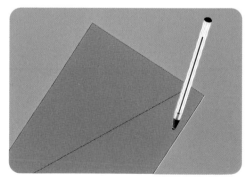

— Fold

5. Lay a ruler on top of the paper from one corner to the other, like this. Draw a dot 1cm (½in) up from the fold, as shown above.

6. Using a hole puncher or a ballpoint pen, make a hole where the dot is. Make sure the hole goes all the way through the paper.

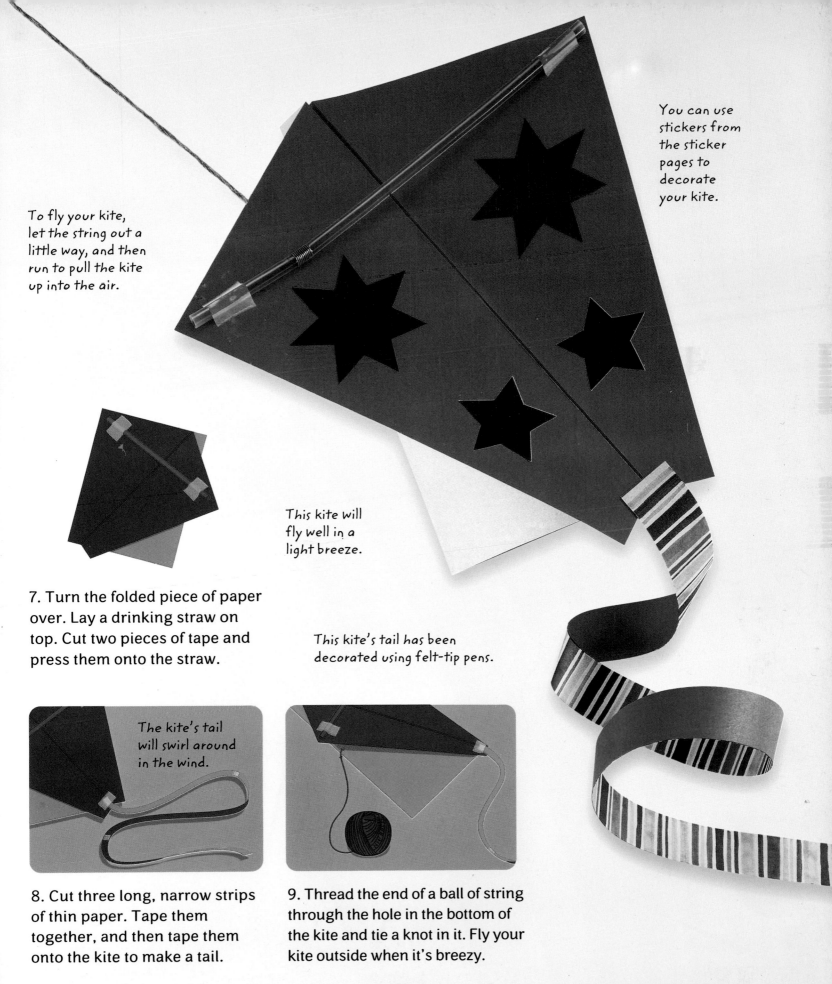

You can use stickers from the sticker pages to decorate your kite.

To fly your kite, let the string out a little way, and then run to pull the kite up into the air.

This kite will fly well in a light breeze.

7. Turn the folded piece of paper over. Lay a drinking straw on top. Cut two pieces of tape and press them onto the straw.

This kite's tail has been decorated using felt-tip pens.

The kite's tail will swirl around in the wind.

8. Cut three long, narrow strips of thin paper. Tape them together, and then tape them onto the kite to make a tail.

9. Thread the end of a ball of string through the hole in the bottom of the kite and tie a knot in it. Fly your kite outside when it's breezy.

45

# Apple-print barn owl

Make the body about twice as long as your hand.

Rinse your spoon after spreading each paint, so they don't mix together.

The stalk of the apple should be at the top.

1. Rip an oval body shape out of brown paper. Rip a piece out of the top to leave two tufty ears. Glue the body onto some blue paper.

2. Put three paper towels on top of an old newspaper. Pour some black, white and orange paint on top. Spread the paint out with a spoon.

3. Cut a small apple in half. Dip one half into the white paint. Press it down near the top of the owl's body to make his face.

You can push a fork into the carrot to use as a handle, if you like.

The carrot prints are the owl's wings.

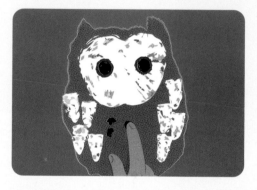

4. Cut the pointed end off a carrot. Cut the end in half. Dip one half into the white paint. Press it onto the owl's body to print a feather.

5. Dip the carrot into the paint again to print more feathers. Print them on the sides of your owl's body, but leave his tummy bare.

6. Fingerpaint two big orange eyes. Let them dry, then fingerpaint the black middles. Add fingerprints for speckles on the owl's tummy.

7. Dip the clean half of the carrot tip into the orange paint. Press it onto the owl's face for a beak. Fingerpaint some orange toes.

You could add blobs of glitter glue for stars in the sky or use star-shaped stickers.

The moon was printed using the thick end of a carrot.

You could give your owl white fingerprints on his tummy as well as black ones.

This owl is sitting on a branch made from ripped paper.

47

# Egg carton spiders

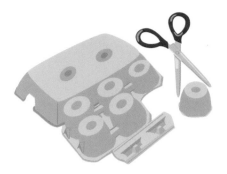

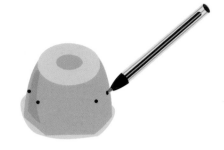

1. Using a pair of scissors, carefully cut one of the corner sections from a cardboard egg carton.

2. Use the tip of a ballpoint pen to push eight small holes around the sides of the section. Make sure the holes are evenly spaced.

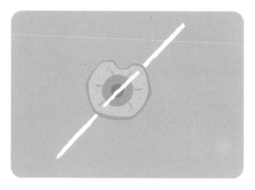

3. For the legs, push a long pipe cleaner in through one of the holes that you made in the side of the section.

4. Push the pipe cleaner out through a hole that is diagonally opposite. Make it the same length on both sides of the section.

5. Do the same with three other pipe cleaners, so that there are eight legs altogether. Then, turn the spider over.

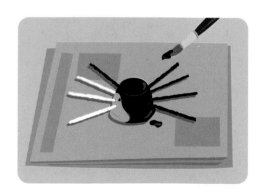

*You can cut out eye shapes from sticky labels, too.*

6. Put the spider onto some newspaper and paint the cardboard and the pipe cleaners black.

7. When the paint is dry, cut out two eyes from pieces of white and black paper and stick them on.

8. Bend each pipe cleaner half way down. Then, bend the tips of the pipe cleaners up to make feet.

If you want to hang your spider up, tape some thread or string to the top.

You could decorate your spider with paper fangs and spots.

49

# Snail-trail letter paper

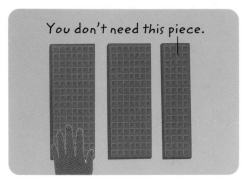

You don't need this piece.

You don't need this piece.

Bend the bottom strip over the top ones to start rolling them up.

1. Cut two strips off a piece of sponge cloth. Make each strip about the same width as your hand.

2. Using a pair of scissors, trim about a third off the top of one of the strips. Then, cut the strip in half lengthways.

3. Lay two small strips on top of the big one, with a gap at each end. Then, start rolling them up, like this.

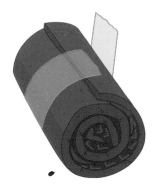

Rinse your spoon between spreading the two paints.

Make sure there isn't too much paint on your roll.

4. Roll the strips all the way up. Then, cut a piece of tape and wrap it around the roll to hold it in place.

5. Pour a little red and a little yellow paint onto an old plate. Spread the paint out with an old spoon.

6. Dip one end of the roll into the yellow paint. Press it onto a piece of paper to print a snail shell.

Once your snail paper is dry, you can use it for writing letters or invitations.

Dear Alice,

Please come to play on Friday after school.

Love from Poppy

Dear Ted,

Thank yo lovely bir present.

Love, Sam

Dear Mrs. Rose,

Please come to my Garden Party on Saturday at 12 o'clock.

Love, Sam

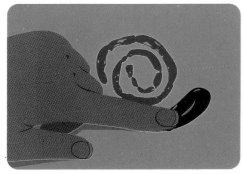

7. Dip the end of the roll into the paint again and print more snail shells around the edges of your piece of paper.

To print a snail facing the other way, use the other end of your sponge roll.

8. Dip your finger into the red paint. Fingerpaint a curvy snail's body. Add the other snails' bodies, too.

9. When the snails are dry, use a felt-tip pen to draw their eyes and mouths. Add feelers on their heads.

If you don't have glitter glue, use normal glue and sprinkle glitter onto it.

10. Squeeze a wavy line of glitter glue leading from the back of each snail. These are their shiny trails.

# Bright bug giftwrap

You will need this piece later.

1. Put a paper towel on top of an old newspaper. Pour red paint on top and spread it out with the back of an old spoon.

2. Cut a small potato in half. Push a fork into one half to use as a handle. Cut the end off the other half of the potato.

3. Dip the half potato into the red paint. Press it onto a big piece of paper to print a bug body. Print lots more bugs in the same way.

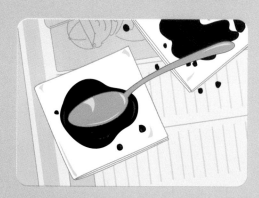

This will be the head.

4. Put another paper towel on top of the newspaper. Pour a little black paint on top and spread it out with a spoon.

5. Push the fork into the cut-off piece of potato. Dip it into the black paint and press it onto each of the bugs' bodies.

6. Dip the tip of your finger into the black paint. Press it onto a bug's back to print a spot. Fingerprint lots more spots on all of the bugs.

7. Wash your hands and let the bugs dry. Then, use a black felt-tip pen to draw a line down the back of each one.

Try fingerpainting stripes on some of your bugs instead of spots.

You could add feelers and eyes to your bugs.

Make sure the giftwrap is dry before using it.

You could cut out a bug to make a gift tag.

# Finger-puppet mice

1. Place a mug on top of a piece of white paper. Draw around it to make a circle. Then, cut the circle out.

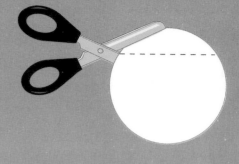

2. Carefully cut a piece the width of two of your fingers off the circle to make a straight edge, like this.

*This one has been folded.*

3. Spread glue halfway along the straight edge. Bend the paper around to make a cone. Hold it until it sticks.

4. Using felt-tip pens, draw a pink nose, black whiskers and two little black eyes on the cone's pointed end.

5. Cut two long ear shapes out of the piece of paper you cut off the circle. Fold their ends over, like this.

6. Fill in the middles of the ears with a pink felt-tip pen. Spread glue under the folds and press them onto the cone.

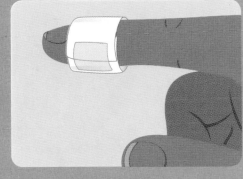

Leave your puppet to dry before you use it.

7. Cut a piece of string for the mouse's tail. Lay the mouse on its back and tape the tail inside the cone.

8. Cut a thin strip of paper and wrap it around your finger. Press a piece of tape on to hold it in place.

9. Put a blob of glue on the rolled-up piece of paper and press it inside the mouse puppet, like this.

# Sam's carrot-print robins

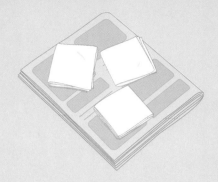

Wash the spoon between spreading each different paint.

Throw this piece away.

1. Fold up three kitchen paper towels and lay them on top of some old newspapers.

2. Pour brown, red and white paint onto the paper towels. Spread the paint with the back of a spoon.

3. Cut a big carrot into four pieces. You don't need to keep the second smallest piece.

4. Press the thickest piece of carrot into the brown paint. Press it onto some paper to print a robin's body.

5. Press the piece of carrot into the paint again and print another body. Do this a few times.

You could paint a log for your robins to sit on.

Press the white circle low on the robin's body.

6. Dip the thinnest end of the medium carrot in white paint. Press it onto the robins' chests.

Draw their footprints as little blue lines in the snow.

7. Dip the smallest piece of carrot into the red paint. Press it onto the white circle on each robin.

8. Leave it to dry, then use a black felt-tip pen to draw the robins' eyes, beaks, legs, wings and tails.

# Mrs. Boot's glittery paper chains

You could use glitter glue instead, if you have it.

Use the left-over glitter to decorate another piece of paper.

1. Dab blobs of glue all over a piece of paper about the size of this page. Sprinkle glitter on top.

2. When the glue is dry, tip the extra glitter onto an old newspaper. Decorate some more paper.

3. When all the glue is dry, cut across the pieces of paper to make lots of short strips.

Make sure the glitter is on the outside.

4. Bend one strip into a loop and tape it into place. Thread another loop through and tape it.

5. Keep on threading and taping loops until you have made a long chain. Hang the chain up.

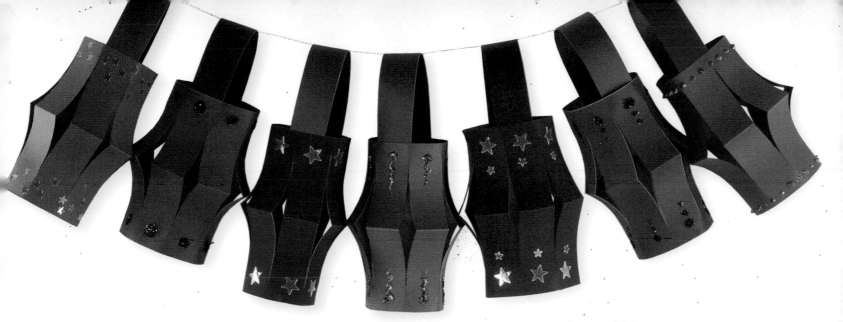

# Ted's paper lanterns

You could decorate your lanterns with silver and gold pens or glitter glue.

Save half of the paper to make another lantern.

Don't cut all the way up to the top.

1. Fold a piece of thick paper about the size of this page in half. Cut down the fold.

2. Fold one piece of paper in half so that the long sides meet. Make cuts along the folded side.

3. Cut the last strip all the way off. Keep it to make the lantern's handle later.

Decorate your lanterns with stickers from the sticker page.

4. Open the paper out. Spread glue along one short edge. Press it onto the other short edge.

5. Put glue on both ends of the strip of paper you cut off in step 3. Press it onto the lantern.

# Stars and icicles

## Star

1. Hold one end of a pipe cleaner against the handle of a thin paintbrush. Wind the rest tightly around the handle.

2. When the whole pipe cleaner is wound around the handle, slide it off. Hold both ends and pull gently to make it a little longer.

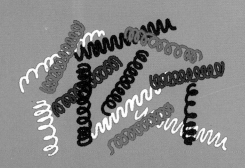

*Make sure the string is in the middle of the pipe cleaners.*

3. Wind more pipe cleaners around the paintbrush in the same way, until you have ten curly pipe cleaners.

4. Lay a piece of thin string on a table. Put the pipe cleaners on top. Tie a tight knot in the middle of the pipe cleaners.

5. Bend all the pipe cleaners away from each other. Tie a knot in the top of the string. Then, hang up your curly star.

# Icicle

1. Bend over the tip of a pipe cleaner. Then, wrap the pipe cleaner tightly around and around itself to make a flat spiral.

2. Hold the outside of the spiral and pull the middle out to make an icicle. Tie a piece of thread around the end and hang it up.

# Bouncing snowman

Make the lines about two finger widths apart.

1. For the body, draw around a large plate on a piece of thin white paper. Cut out the circle you have drawn and fold it in half.

2. Draw a line from the fold of the circle almost to the edge. Then, draw one from the edge almost to the fold, like this.

3. Draw another line coming from the fold almost to the edge. Make this two finger widths below the second line.

4. Continue to draw lines from the fold, then from the edge. Then, cut along the pencil lines, keeping the paper folded.

5. Unfold the circle and flatten it. Then, draw around a saucer for the head. Cut it out and glue it onto the body.

6. Cut a hat from a piece of black paper and glue it on. Draw on eyes and a mouth with felt-tip pens, and glue on a paper nose.

Glue buttons, cut from paper, on the snowman's body.

To make your snowman bounce, pull one of its boots gently, then let go.

This snowman's scarf was made from strips of paper.

7. Cut out arms, like sticks, from black paper and glue them on the back of the body. Cut out boots and glue them on, too.

8. Cut a piece of thread or ribbon and tape it to the back of the hat. Hold the snowman's hat and gently pull the body to stretch it.

9. Before you hang your snowman press some poster tack onto the bottom of the body. This will help it bounce.

63

# Sparkly snowflakes

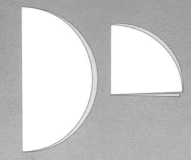

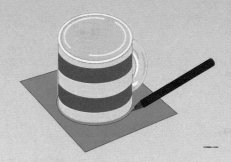

1. Put a mug on top of a piece of white paper. Use a pencil to draw around the mug.

2. Cut out the circle you have drawn. Fold it in half, and then fold it in half again.

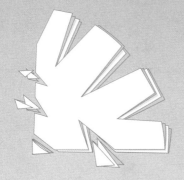

3. Using a pair of scissors, cut little shapes out of the paper. Cut a tiny piece off the pointed end, too.

4. Open out the circle to see the cut-out snowflake. Glue sequins and glitter onto it.

5. Put the mug on a piece of tissue paper. Draw around it. Then, cut out the circle of tissue paper.

6. Put dots of glue on the back of the snowflake and press the tissue onto it. Tape it in a window.